# THE

# "ZUCCHINI LOVERS COOKBOOK"

BY: ADDIE GONSHOROWSKI

ISBN: 0-9600982-4-0

## ACKNOWLEDGEMENT

Special thanks to my relatives and friends for sharing their treasured recipes. And to my family for all their help and support.

## TO

STAN, My husband

## COVER BY

Linus Maurer
San Francisco, Ca.

## PUBLISHED BY

ADDIE'S RECIPE BOX
DRAWER 5426-Z79
EUGENE, OREGON 97405

# CONTENTS

# NOTICE

Author and/or publisher not responsible for anything beyond the price of one book.

# ZUCCHINI-SAUCE CAKE

1 cup margarine
2 cups sugar
3 cups Zucchini-sauce
4 tsp soda
2 tsp cloves
1 tsp nutmeg
1-1/2 cups raisins - Soaked & drained.

1 tsp allspice
1 tsp salt
3 cups flour
2 eggs
1/2 cup nuts,chop
2 tsp cinnamon

Cream margarine & sugar. ADD eggs. Combine
dry ingredients. Add alternately with
Zucchini-sauce. Add raisins & nuts.

Pour into 2 greased & floured 9" pans.
Sprinkle tops with mixture of 1/4 cup
sugar & 1/2 tsp cinnamon.. BAKE 350
degrees about 1 hour to done.

SERVE slightly warmed with Ice cream.

# BUTTERSCOTCH CAKE

1-1/2 cups sugar
1/2 cup butter
2 eggs
2 cups flour
1 tsp vanilla
1 cup Zucchini-sauce
2/3 cup butterscotch chips

1 tsp soda
2 tsp cinnamon
1/2 tsp cloves
1/2 tsp salt
1/2 cup nuts

CREAM butter & sugar. ADD eggs & vanilla.
Beat well.. Mix dry ingredients & add
alternately with Zucchini-sauce. Mix well.

Stir in rest of ingredients. Bake in 9 X
13" greased,floured pan 350 for 35 minutes.

TOPPING: Mix 1/3 cup butterscotch bits, 2
tblsp butter, 1/2 cup coconut, 1/3 cup
brown sugar, 1/4 cup light cream. HEAT
to melted. SPREAD on baked, slightly
cool cake & broil until bubbles form.

SERVE slightly warm with Ice cream.

(Zucchini-Sauce recipe page 86)

5

# CHOCOLATE CHIP CAKE

| | |
|---|---|
| 1/2 cup margarine | 2-1/2 cup flour |
| 1/2 cup melted shortening | 1/4 tsp salt |
| 1-3/4 cup sugar | 4 tblsp cocoa |
| 2 eggs | 1/4 tsp soda |
| 2 tsp vinegar | 1 tsp cinnamon |
| 1 tsp vanilla | 1/2 tsp cloves |
| 1/2 tsp baking powder | 1/2 cup milk |

1/4 cup minature chocolate chips
2 cups finely diced peeled Zucchini

Add vinegar to milk & let set 15 minutes.

Cream margarine, melted shortening and sugar.

Add eggs, vanilla and milk. MIX WELL.

Mix flour, baking powder, salt, cocoa, soda, cinnamon, cloves.

Add to creamed mixture & beat well.

Stir in Zucchini and chocolate chips.

Bake in 9" X 12" pan which has been greased & floured for 40 to 45 minutes at 350 degrees.


## GLAZE

Mix 1/2 cup powder sugar and enough milk or cream to make a thin glaze.

Beat well and drizzle over cool cake.

Serve slightly warm with Ice cream.

# APPLEBUTTER CAKE

1/2 cup butter,melted
1/2 cup applebutter
1/2 cup Zucchini-sauce
1-1/2 cups flour
1 tsp cinnamon
1/2 cup raisins
3/4 cup packed brown
                sugar

1 egg
1 tsp vanilla
1/2 tsp cloves
1/4 tsp nutmeg
1/4 tsp allspice
1/2 tsp salt
1 tsp soda

Soak raisins in hot water 4 minutes. DRAIN

Combine butter, sugar, applebutter, egg, vanilla & Zucchini-sauce (Recipe page 86)

Mix together flour, soda, salt, cinnamon, cloves, nutmeg and allspice.

Add to butter mixture & mix well. Add raisins.

Pour into greased 9" square pan and sprinkle lightly with sugar then with the following topping.

TOPPING

Combine:  3 tblsp sugar - 3 tblsp brown sugar, packed - 3 tblsp flour - 1/4 tsp cinnamon - 1/4 tsp nutmeg - 3 tblsp soft butter- and 1/2 cup chopped nuts.

Mix until crumbly and sprinkle over batter.

Bake 350 degrees 40 to 50 minutes or until toothpick comes out clean when inserted in center.

Serve slightly warmed with Ice cream or whipped cream.

# PRUNE SPICE CAKE

| | |
|---|---|
| 1 cup prunes | 1 cup flour |
| 1 cup Zucchini | 1-1/2 cups sugar |
| 1/2 cup cooking oil | 1-1/4 tsp soda |
| 3 eggs | 1 tsp salt |
| 1-1/2 tsp cinnamon | 1 tsp nutmeg |
| 1/2 tsp cloves | |

Peel & chop fine the Zucchini. Place in saucepan and add 2 cups water; Cook 10 minutes; Add pitted prunes and cook to tender or about 15 minutes longer.

Drain and reserve 2/3 cup of the liquid. Chop the prunes fine.

In mixer bowl combine flour, sugar, soda, salt, cinnamon, cloves & nutmeg.

Add prune liquid & oil & mix low speed to blend.. Then beat medium 2 minutes.

Add eggs and beat 1 minute longer.

Stir in prunes and Zucchini.

Pour into greased and floured 7" X 12" baking dish.

Sprinkle with topping and bake 350 degrees about 35 minutes or to done.

## TOPPING

Combine 1/2 cup sugar, 2 tblsp flour, 2 tblsp butter, 1 tsp cinnamon

MIX until crumbly.

ADD 1/2 cup fine chopped nuts.

Serve cake warm with whip cream or Ice cream.

# GERMAN CHOCOLATE CAKE

1/2 cup margarine
3/4 cup sugar
2 tblsp hot water
2 oz German chocolate
1-1/2 tsp baking powder
3/4 cup shredded Zucchini,
      Partly drained

2 eggs
1 cup flour
1/4 tsp salt
1/3 cup nuts
2 tblsp flour


Melt chocolate

Mix zucchini, nuts and 2 tblsp flour to coat well.

Cream margarine and sugar.

Add hot water and continue beating

Add eggs, and chocolate

Combine 1 cup flour, baking powder and salt.

Add slowly beating as you add.

Add zucchini and nuts to mixture.

Bake in greased and floured 8 X 8" pan 350 degrees about 40 minutes to done.

Serve slightly warmed with Ice cream or whip cream.

# PINEAPPLE CARROT CAKE

1 cup shortening  
2-1/2 cups cake flour  
1 tsp baking powder  
1 cup chopped nuts  
2 cups ground raw carrots  
1/2 cup shredded Zucchini, Partly drained  
1/2 cup crushed pineapple, well drained  
1/2 cup pineapple juice  

2 cups sugar  
4 eggs, beaten  
1 tsp soda  
2 tsp cinnamon  

Beat sugar and shortening to fluffy.

Add eggs and beat.

Mix flour, baking powder, soda and cinnamon.

Add alternately to creamed mixture with pineapple juice.

Beat well.

Add carrots, zucchini, pineapple & nuts.

Bake in 9" X 13" pan 350 degrees about 40 minutes or to done.


## FROSTING

Cream 1 (8 oz) pkg soft cream cheese, 1/2 cup margarine and 1 lb powder sugar.

Add 1/4 cup drained crushed pineapple.

# HONEY CAKE

| | |
|---|---|
| 1 tblsp vinegar | 2-1/2 cups flour |
| 3/4 cup milk | 3 tsp baking powder |
| 1 cup cooking oil | 1/2 tsp soda |
| 1-1/2 cups sugar | 1-1/2 tsp cinnamon |
| 3 eggs | 1/4 tsp cloves |
| 1 tsp vanilla | 1/2 cup chopped nuts |

1 cup shredded zucchini, drained well

Mix vinegar and milk and let set.

Mix oil, sugar, eggs, and vanilla.

Beat 1 minute on medium speed.

Mix dry ingredients and add alternately with milk to oil mixture.

Beat 1 minute. Stir in nuts & zucchini.

Bake in greased tube pan 350 degrees about 50 minutes.

Cool. Prick holes in cake and drizzle with following syrup.

## SYRUP:

Boil together 1/4 cup honey, 1 tblsp water and 1 tblsp lemon juice.

Serve cake slightly warm with Ice cream or whipped cream.

# PINEAPPLE CAKE

3 eggs            1 tsp salt
2 cups sugar      1 tsp soda
2 tblsp vanilla    1 tsp cinnamon
1 cup cooking oil   1/2 cup nuts, chop
3 cups flour       1/2 cup raisins
1 tsp baking powder

1 cup crushed pineapple, drained
2 cups peeled shredded or ground coarsely
Zucchini, Drained well.

Beat eggs until fluffy.

Add sugar, vanilla, oil & Zucchini.

Mix together flour, baking powder, salt,
soda and cinnamon.

Add to egg mixture.

Add pineapple, nuts and raisins.

Bake in 2 - 8 X 8" greased pans 325
degrees about 1 hour or until done.

## FROSTING

8 oz soft cream cheese
1/2 cup margarine
1 pound powder sugar
1/2 cup crushed pineapple, drained.

Beat until smooth cream cheese,
margarine and powder sugar.

Add pineapple.

Spread between layers & sides and
on top of the cake.

# COCOA CAKE

2-1/2 cups flour
2/3 cup cocoa
2-1/2 tsp baking powder
1-1/2 tsp cinnamon
3/4 cup margarine
1/2 cups chopped nuts
1 tsp grated orange peel
2 cups Zucchini, coarsely shredded

1-1/2 tsp soda
1 tsp salt
2 cups sugar
3 eggs
2 tsp vanilla
1/2 cup milk

Combine flour, cocoa, baking powder, soda, salt and cinnamon.

Beat together to smooth margarine and sugar.

Add eggs 1 at a time and beat.

Stir in vanilla, peel and Zucchini.

Stir in dry ingredients alternately with milk. Then add the nuts.

Bake in greased and floured 10" tube pan 350 degrees about 1 hour to done.

Cool 15 minutes before turning out.

## FROSTING

Mix: 2 cups powder sugar, 1 tsp vanilla
     2 tblsp butter & enough milk to
     make a thin glaze.

BEAT to smooth and drizzle over cake.

BY:  Evelyn Parsen
     Pierre, So. Dak.

# CARROT CAKE

2-1/2 cups flour          2 cups sugar
1 cup shortening          1 tsp soda
4 eggs, beaten            2 tsp cinnamon
1 tsp baking powder       1/4 cup water
2 cups ground raw carrots
2/3 cup ground peeled Zucchini, drained
1 cup fine chopped walnuts

Beat sugar and shortening to fluffy.

Add eggs & beat. Alternately add dry
ingredients & water. Beat well. Add
carrots, Zucchini and nuts. Stir well.

Bake in 2 - 8 X 8" greased pans 350
degrees about 40 minutes.

Serve slightly warm with whipped cream
or Ice cream OR FROST

FROSTING:

MIX TOGETHER: 8 oz soft cream cheese,
1/2 cup margarine and 1 lb powder sugar.

Beat to smooth.


# HOW TO WARM FOODS

CAKES: Wrap in aluminum foil and place
        in hot oven for few minutes.


TEA BREADS: Slice & spread with butter
        and place under broiler until
        butter is melted and slices are
        warm.

14

# PUMPKIN RING

1-1/2 cups sugar
1/2 cup margarine
2 eggs
2 cups flour
1 tsp baking powder
1/2 tsp soda
1 cup canned pumpkin
1-1/2 cups peeled shredded Zucchini,
      Drain well.

1/4 tsp salt
1/2 tsp cinnamon
1/2 tsp nutmeg
1/4 tsp cloves
1/4 tsp ginger
1/2 cup nuts

Cream margarine, sugar & add eggs 1 at a time. Beat well after each. Blend in pumpkin.

Mix together dry ingredients, zucchini & nuts. Add to mixture & stir well.

Bake in greased & floured 8" tube pan 350 degrees 55 minutes. Cool 10 minutes. Turn out & sprinkle with powder sugar.

# ORANGE CAKE

1 Orange
1 cup raisins
1/3 cup nuts
2 cups flour
1 tsp soda
1 cup shredded zucchini, well drained.

1 tsp salt
1 cup sugar
2/3 cup milk
1/2 cup shortening
2 eggs

Juice the orange & save. Grind rind, pulp with raisins & nuts. SET ASIDE

Mix dry ingredients & add milk, eggs & shortening. Beat 4 minutes.

Fold in ground mixture & zucchini.

Bake in greased 9 X 13" pan 350 degrees about 45 minutes.. While still warm spread top with the juice. Sprinkle with powder sugar & cinnamon. Serve slightly warm.

# BLUEBERRY CAKE

1 cup sugar
1/2 cup butter
2 tsp baking powder
2 tsp cinnamon
1 cup zucchini, finely chopped
1 cup fresh or frozen blueberries

2 cups flour
2 eggs
1/4 tsp salt
1 cup milk

Cream butter & add sugar slowly. Beat & add eggs 1 at a time. Beat well. Mix dry ingredients & add alternately with milk.

Sprinkle additional 1/2 cup flour over zucchini & berries then fold into batter.

Pour into greased 9" pan & sprinkle with mixture of sugar & cinnamon and bake 350 degrees about 30 minutes to done.

Serve slightly warm with whip cream.

# BANANA CAKE

1/2 cup shortening
1 cup mashed banana
1/2 cup apple juice
2-1/2 cups flour
1/2 tsp baking powder
2/3 cup raisins
1 cup Zucchini-sauce
    (See page 86)

1-1/2 tsp soda
3 tsp cinnamon
1/2 tsp cloves
1/2 tsp allspice
3/4 tsp salt
2 eggs
1/2 cup nuts
2 cups sugar

Mix dry ingredients; Add juice, banana, shortening & sauce. Beat at medium speed to creamy. Add eggs & beat 2 minutes. Stir in nuts and raisins.

Pour into wax paper lined 9 X 13" pan and bake 350 degrees about 45 minutes.

Turn out of pan & dust top with powder sugar. Serve warm with Ice cream.

# CARROT MOLASSES CAKE

1/2 cup butter
1 cup hot water
3/4 cup light molasses
1/3 cup carrots
1/3 cup zucchini
1 egg
3/4 cup packed brown sugar

2-1/2 cups flour
2 tsp soda
1 tsp cinnamon
1 tsp ginger
1 tsp nutmeg
1/2 tsp salt

Peel & shred carrots and zucchini.

Cream butter and sugar. Add egg and molasses and beat together.

Mix flour, soda, and spices.

Add dry ingredients alternately with hot water to creamed mixture and beat well.

Stir in carrots and zucchini.

Bake 350 degree oven in greased & flour 8" square pan for 45 to 55 minutes or until done.

Serve with lemon sauce below.


## LEMON SAUCE

Melt 1/4 cup butter. Stir 1 tblsp cornstarch & 1 cup sugar together, then add to butter. mix well.

Stir in 1-1/4 cup water slowly. Add 1/2 tsp grated lemon rind and bring to boil. Cook 3 minutes. Add 1-1/2 tblsp lemon juice.

Serve warm over warmed cake.

# DATE CAKE

1 cup boiling water    1 egg
1 cup chopped dates    1 tsp vanilla
1 tsp soda    1/2 tsp cloves
1/2 cup white sugar    1 tsp soda
1/2 cup shortening    1/2 tsp salt
1-1/2 tsp cinnamon    1-1/2 cup flour
1/2 cup brown sugar, packed
1 cup Zucchini, peeled and shredded.

Mix Zucchini and dates. Stir in soda and boiling water. LET SET TO COOL

Cream shortening and sugars - Add egg and vanilla and beat to fluffy

Mix flour, salt, cinnamon and cloves.

Stir cooled Zucchini mixture into creamed mixture.

Add dry ingredients and beat well.

Pour into greased and floured 9" X 11" cake pan.

Bake 350 degrees 35 to 45 minutes or until done.

Spread with topping below.

## TOPPING

Mix 1/4 cup butter, 1/4 cup milk, 1/2 cup brown sugar & 1 cup shredded coconut.

Spread over top of hot cake & place under broiler until bubbly.. Watch carefully.

Serve cake warm with Ice cream.

# PINTO BEAN CAKE

| | |
|---|---|
| 1/2 cup white sugar | 1 egg |
| 1/4 cup margarine | 1/2 tsp salt |
| 1-1/2 cups flour | 1 tsp soda |
| 2 tsp cinnamon | 1/2 tsp cloves |
| 1 cup chopped nuts | 1/2 tsp allspice |
| 1 tsp vanilla | 1 cup raisins |

1/2 cup packed brown sugar
2 cups Pinto Beans, canned - Drain and
  mash
2 cups peeled, seeded, chopped Zucchini.

Cream sugars and margarine. ADD egg.

Sift together flour, cinnamon, salt,
soda, cloves and allspice.

Mix beans, nuts, zucchini, raisins,
and vanilla together.

To the creamed mixture add the flour
mixture then the zucchini mixture.

Bake in greased and floured pan 350
degrees about 1 hour and 15 minutes
or until done.

Serve warm with whip cream or Ice cream.

NOTE: Raisins may be soaked in hot
      water for 5 minutes and then
      drained to make them more plump.

19

# PINEAPPLE BRAN MUFFINS

1/3 cup Zucchini milk
1 cup crushed pineapple
1/4 cup shortening
2 tsp baking powder
1 cup All-Bran cereal
3 tblsp evaporated milk
1/2 cup brown sugar, dark kind,
    firmly packed

1 cup flour
1/2 tsp salt
1/4 tsp soda
1/4 cup rasins
1 egg

Beat shortening and egg.

Add bran, Zucchini-milk, evaporated milk, pineapple and raisins.

Mix well on very slow speed.

Mix flour, baking powder, sugar, salt and soda.

Add flour mixture to first mixture and fold in just until flour is dampened.

Spoon into greased or paper lined muffin cups.

Bake 400 degrees about 20 to 30 minutes.

(Zucchini-milk recipe page 60)

# CRANBERRY MUFFINS

1/2 cup butter
1 cup sugar
2 tsp baking powder
1 tsp cinnamon

2 cups flour
1/4 tsp salt
2 eggs
1 cup milk

1 cup raw chopped cranberries
1 cup Zucchini, peeled, cored and chopped very fine.

Cream butter and sugar until fluffy

Add eggs and beat well.

Mix flour, baking powder, salt and cinnamon.

Alternately add dry ingredients with milk to creamed mixture.

In separate bowl place cranberries and zucchini. Sprinkle with 1/2 cup flour and stir to coat the pieces.

Add cranberries and zucchini to mixture.

Bake in greased muffin pans 350 degrees about 30 minutes or until done.

Sprinkle with powder sugar and cinnamon mixture.

Serve slightly warm with butter.

# PINEAPPLE UPSIDE DOWN MUFFINS

1/3 cup brown sugar, packed
1/4 tsp lemon extract
3 tsp baking powder
1-1/2 tsp cinnamon
1/4 tsp nutmeg
1/2 tsp salt
3 cups flour
1 beaten egg
1 cup milk
3 tblsp oil
3 tblsp butter, melted
1/4 cup white sugar
1 cup zucchini, peeled, seeded & chopped
1 cup crushed, drained pineapple


Combine brown sugar, lemon extract, 1/8 tsp nutmeg, butter, pineapple & Zucchini.

Divide into 16 greased muffin pans.

In separate bowl mix flour, white sugar, baking powder, salt, 1/8 tsp nutmeg and cinnamon.

Combine cooking oil, egg and milk

Add egg mixture all at once to dry ingredients and stir quickly to just moistened.

Spoon into muffin pans on top of the zucchini mixture.

Bake 400 degrees 18 to 20 minutes or until done.

Turn out of pans immediately.

Serve slightly warm

# DATE MUFFINS

2 cups flour                   1/2 tsp salt
4 tsp baking powder            1 egg, beaten
1-1/2 tsp cinnamon
2 tblsp packed brown sugar
1/2 cup evaporated milk
1/2 cup Zucchini-milk
1/4 cup melted butter
3/4 cup chopped dates


MIX flour, salt, sugar, baking powder
and cinnamon in large bowl.

In separate bowl mix milk, Zucchini-milk,
butter and egg.

Add to flour mixture and stir just to
moisten.

Fold in dates.

Fill greased muffin pans 2/3 full.

Bake 400 degrees about 20 to 30 minutes.

Turn out and serve warm with butter.

Also, good served with jam.


( How to make Zucchini-milk)
(See page 60)

# CHOCOLATE CHIP BARS

1/2 cup margarine          1 egg
2 tsp grated lemon rind    1/4 tsp soda
1-1/4 cups flour           1/4 tsp salt
1 tsp vanilla              1/2 cup nuts
3/4 cup brown sugar, firmly packed
1/2 cup raisins
1 cup Zucchini,finely chopped
1/2 cup chocolate chips, minature size


Cream margarine & brown sugar.

Add egg, vanilla and lemon rind.

Mix together in separate bowl the flour, soda and salt.

Add gradually to creamed mixture stirring to mix well.

Add nuts, raisins, Zucchini and chocolate chips and mix well.

Spread in greased 9 X 13" pan.

Bake 350 degrees about 30 minutes or until light brown.

Cool and cut into bars.


**NOTE:** If desired frost with a powder sugar glaze.

# CHOCOLATE CHIP COOKIES

3/4 cup butter          3-1/4 cups flour
1-1/2 cups sugar        2 tsp cinnamon
1 egg                   1/2 tsp salt
1-1/2 tsp vanilla       2 tsp baking powder

1-1/2 cups fine ground zucchini,
1/2 cup coarsely chopped nuts
3/4 cup miniature chocolate chips

Cream butter & sugar. Beat in egg and
vanilla. Mix in zucchini.

Mix dry ingredients and add.. Stir in
nuts and chocolate chips.

Drop on greased sheets. Bake 350 degrees
about 15 minutes. Cool on racks.

# RAISIN NUT COOKIES

7 tblsp margarine       1/2 tsp cloves
1 egg, beaten           1/2 tsp salt
2 cups flour            1 tsp vanilla
1 tsp soda              3/4 cup nuts
1-1/2 tsp cinnamon      3/4 cup raisins

1 cup brown sugar, firmly packed
1 cup fine ground peeled zucchini

Cream margarine & sugar. Add egg, vanilla
and zucchini.

Mix dry ingredients & add to mixture.

Add rest of ingredients & mix well.

Drop on greased sheets and bake 375
degrees about 12 minutes to done.

# ZUCCHINI SAUCE BARS

1/2 cup shortening
1 cup sugar
1-1/2 cups flour
1 tsp cinnamon
1 egg, slightly beaten
1 cup thick Zucchini sauce (Page 86)

1 tsp soda
1/8 tsp cloves
1/4 tsp salt
1/2 cup raisins

Cream shortening & sugar. Add egg and Zucchini.. Mix together rest of ingredients and add to batter. Mix well.

Bake in 9 X 12" pan 350 for 35 minutes.

FROSTING; Melt 1/2 sq. unsweet chocolate. Stir in 3 tblsp butter & 2 tblsp milk.

Cool and beat in 1 cup powder sugar to make a glaze. Spread on bars. Sprinkle with nuts & coconut before cutting.

# BANANA COOKIES

1 cup shortening
1/2 cup buttermilk
2 eggs
1 tsp vanilla
1 cup mashed bananas
1/2 cup chopped nuts
1 cup fine chopped Zucchini

3 cups flour
1 cup sugar
1/2 tsp soda
1-1/2 tsp cinnamon
1/2 cup raisins

Cream shortening & sugar; Add eggs; Beat.

Mix dry ingredients. Add alternately with buttermilk & bananas. Add raisins and nuts. Add Zucchini.

Drop on greased cookie sheets and bake 350 degrees about 15 to 20 minutes or until light brown.

# APPLEBUTTER COOKIES

1/2 cup margarine
1 cup quick rolled oats
1 tsp baking powder
1/2 cup raisins
1 cup apple butter
1/3 cup packed brown sugar
1 cup zucchini, very finely chopped

1 cup flour
1/2 tsp salt
2 eggs
1/2 cup nuts

Cream margarine; Add sugar & beat fluffy.

Add eggs one at a time and beat. Add applebutter. Mix well.

Combine dry ingredients & add to creamed mixture. Add rest of ingredients & mix.

Drop on greased sheets and bake 350 degrees about 15 to 18 minutes to done.

# CINNAMON COOKIES

3/4 cup melted shortening
2 eggs, lightly beaten
1/2 cup brown sugar, packed
1 cup white sugar
1 tsp baking powder
2 tsp cinnamon
1/2 cup raisins (Soak 5 minutes & Drain)
1-1/2 cups zucchini, medium fine grind.

3 cups flour
1/2 tsp soda
1/2 tsp salt
1/2 cup nuts
2 tsp vanilla

Beat eggs & sugar. Add shortening.

Stir in zucchini. Mix dry ingredients & add to mixture. Add rest of ingredients.

Mix well and chill for several hours
Drop on greased sheets and bake 350 degrees 12 to 15 minutes.

Do  not overbake.

# GRANOLA COOKIES

3/4 cup margarine
1-1/2 cup brown sugar
    firmly packed
1 egg
1-1/2 cups flour
3/4 tsp orange extract
3 cups granola cereal
1/2 tsp grated orange rind
1 cup Zucchini, medium fine ground

1 tsp vanilla
1/2 tsp allspice
2 tsp cinnamon
1 tsp salt
1 tsp soda
3/4 cup raisins
1/2 cup nuts

BEAT margarine & sugar.. ADD egg, vanilla, orange extract & rind.

ADD Zucchini. MIX dry ingredients and add to creamed mixture. ADD rest of ingredients

DROP on greased cookie sheets and bake 375 degrees about 12 to 15 minutes.

# GLAZED PINEAPPLE COOKIES

1 cup sugar
1 egg
1-1/2 cup margarine
1 tsp baking powder
1/2 cup chopped nuts
1/2 cup crushed pineapple, drained
1/2 cup shredded peeled Zucchini, drained.

4 cups flour
1 tsp vanilla
1 pkg pineapple
        jello

Cream margarine; ADD sugar & jello. BEAT.

ADD egg & vanilla & beat. ADD pineapple & Zucchini. MIX rest of ingredients & add.

DROP on ungreased sheets & bake 400 degrees 12 minutes to done. Cool & glaze. :.

GLAZE MIX together 1 cup sifted powder sugar & 2 tblsp pineapple juice to smooth.

# ORANGE BARS

2-1/3 cups flour
1/2 tsp orange extract
1/4 cup molasses
1 cup Zucchini-sauce
1/2 cup butter
2 eggs
1 tblsp grated orange peel
1/2 cup chopped nuts

1 tsp soda
1 tsp cinnamon
1/2 tsp nutmeg
1/2 tsp salt
1 cup sugar

Mix flour, soda, cinnamon, nutmeg & salt.

Cream butter & sugar. Beat in molasses.

Add eggs and beat until light.

Add flour mixture, zucchini-sauce, orange peel and orange extract.

Gently stir just to blend. Add nuts.

Pour into 3 greased 8" X 8" baking pans.

Bake 350 degrees about 30 minutes or to done. COOL & GLAZE.


## ORANGE GLAZE

Beat 3 cups powder sugar and 3 to 6 tblsp orange juice to smooth.

Spread over bars and sprinkle top with chopped nuts.

Cut into bars.

(Zucchini-sauce recipe page 86)

# CRUNCHY TOP BARS

1 cup sugar
1/2 cup shortening
1 cup Zucchini-sauce
   (see page 86)
1 cup raisins
1/2 cup nuts
1/4 cup sugar
1/2 cup crushed cornflakes
2 tblsp butter, melted

2 cups flour
1 tsp soda
2 tsp cinnamon
1 tsp nutmeg
1/4 tsp cloves
1/2 tsp salt
1 tsp vanilla

Soak raisins in hot water 5 minutes then drain well.

Cream 1 cup sugar and shortening until light and fluffy.

Add Zucchini-sauce and vanilla.

Combine flour, soda, cinnamon, nutmeg, cloves and salt.

Add to sugar mixture and blend well.

Add raisins.

Pour into greased 10" X 15" pan.

Combine the cornflakes, nuts, 1/4 cup sugar and melted butter.

Mix to blend well and sprinkle over batter.

Bake 350 degrees about 25 minutes or until done.

Cool and cut into bars.

# FROSTED MAPLE COOKIES

| | |
|---|---|
| 1/2 cup shortening | 1/2 tsp soda |
| 1 cup brown sugar, packed | 1 tsp salt |
| 1/2 cup white sugar | 1/2 cup nuts |
| 1 tblsp maple flavoring | 2 eggs |
| 2-3/4 cup flour | 1 cup sour |
| 1 cup Zucchini, Shred coarse | cream |

Cream shortening, sugars & eggs. Add cream & flavoring. Beat in dry ingredients. Add well drained zucchini & chopped nuts.

Drop on greased sheets & bake 375 degrees 10 to 12 minutes. Remove & cool.. Frost.

FROSTING: Heat 1/2 cup margarine until golden brown: Blend in 2 cups powder sugar; Add 2 tsp maple flavor. Stir in 2 to 4 tblsp hot water to spread well.

# BLUEBERRY COOKIES

| | |
|---|---|
| 1/2 cup butter | 1 cup sugar |
| 2-1/4 cup flour | 2 tsp cinnamon |
| 1 tsp lemon juice | 1/2 tsp salt |
| 1 tsp lemon rind, grated | 1/4 cup milk |
| 2 tsp baking powder | 1 egg |
| 1 cup Zucchini, chopped fine | |
| 1 cup blueberries, frozen | |

Beat butter; gradually add sugar; Beat to smooth; Beat in rind, juice and egg.

Mix dry ingredients and add alternately with milk. Stir in Zucchini & Blueberries.

Drop on greased sheets and bake 375 degrees about 15 minutes to golden brown.

Remove from pans to racks and dust with powder sugar.

# PUMPKIN COOKIES

2 cups sugar
2 cups shortening
2 eggs
2 tsp vanilla
2 tsp baking powder
1/2 tsp allspice
1 - 16 oz can pumpkin

4 cups flour
1 tsp soda
2 tsp cinnamon
1 tsp salt
1 tsp nutmeg
1/2 cup nuts
2 cups raisins

2 cups Zucchini, shredded & drained well.

CREAM shortening & sugar. ADD pumpkin, eggs & vanilla. Add flour & spices. Stir in rest of ingredients & drop on greased sheets.

BAKE 350 degrees 12 minutes. Frost if desired with your favorite glaze.

# BUTTERSCOTCH COOKIES

1 tsp baking powder
1/2 tsp cloves
1/2 tsp nutmeg
1 tsp cinnamon
1/2 cups raisins

2 cups flour
1/2 tsp salt
1/4 cup milk
1/2 cup nuts
2 eggs

1-1/4 cup brown sugar packed
1/2 cup soft margarine
1 cup Zucchini, Peeled & very fine chop.
1/2 pkg miniature butterscotch bits.

Cream sugar & margarine. ADD eggs & milk.

Mix dry ingredients & add. Then stir in rest of ingredients.

Drop on greased sheets and bake 375 degrees about 12 minutes.

# LEMON MOLASSES COOKIES

1/3 cup shortening        1 egg
1/2 cup sugar              3 cups flour
1/2 cup light molasses    3/4 tsp soda
1/2 tsp lemon extract     1 tsp ginger
                          1/2 tsp salt
1 cup Zucchini, peel, shred and drain.

Cream shortening & sugar. Stir in molasses, egg and extract.

Mix together dry ingredients & add to creamed mixture. FOLD in Zucchini.

Form into balls & place on greased sheets. Flatten

Bake 350 degrees about 12 minutes.


# ZUCCHINI SAUCE COOKIES

1 cup raisins             1 egg
1 cup Zucchini sauce      2 cups flour
1 cup packed brown sugar 1/2 tsp salt
1/2 cup shortening       1/2 tsp nutmeg
1 cup chopped nuts      1 tsp soda
2 tsp cinnamon          1/4 tsp cloves

Mix raisins with Zucchini sauce. Let set.

Mix sugar, shortening & egg. Beat well.

Mix dry ingredients. Combine mixtures.

Add nuts.

Drop on greased sheets and bake 375 degrees about 13 minutes

( ZUCCHINI SAUCE RECIPE PAGE 86)

# MOLASSES COOKIES

| | |
|---|---|
| 1/2 cup shortening | 3 cups flour |
| 1/2 cup sugar | 1 tsp cinnamon |
| 1 egg, beat slightly | 3/4 tsp cloves |
| 3/4 cup molasses | 1/2 tsp ginger |
| 1 tsp lemon extract | 2 tsp soda |
| 1/2 tsp butter extract | 1/8 tsp salt |
| 1 cup Zucchini - Peeled & chopped fine. | |

Cream shortening & sugar. Stir in molasses egg and flavorings. BLEND WELL.

Mix dry ingredients & add to mixture.

Stir in rest of the ingredients.

Drop on greased cookie sheets.
Bake 350 degrees about 17 minutes.

**BY:** Carolyn Gonshorowski, Eugene, Oregon

# RAISIN SPICE COOKIES

| | |
|---|---|
| 1/2 cup shortening | 2 cups flour |
| 1-1/3 cup brown sugar, packed | 1/2 tsp nutmeg |
| | 1/2 tsp salt |
| 1 egg | 1 tsp soda |
| 1/4 cup milk | 1 tsp cinnamon |
| 1 cup raisins | 1 tsp cloves |
| 3/4 cup Zucchini, Chop very fine | 1 cup nuts |

Cream shortening, sugar. Add egg & beat.

Mix dry ingredients & stir in with milk.

Add rest of ingredients.

Drop on greased pans & bake 400 degrees about 12 minutes to done.

While hot glaze with your favorite frosting.

34

# DATE BARS

1 cup dates
1 cup Zucchini
1/4 cup white sugar
1 cup lemonade
1/2 tsp salt

1-1/2 cups flour
1-1/2 cups quick
  oatmeal, uncooked
1/2 cup brown sugar
3/4 cup butter
1/2 cup nuts

In saucepan cook chopped dates and
chopped peeled zucchini, with the sugar,
lemonade and 1/4 tsp salt.

Simmer until thick.

Add chopped nuts

In separate bowl combine flour, oats,
packed brown sugar and 1/4 tsp salt.

Cut in butter until crumbly

Pat 1/2 of oat mixture in greased
9" X 9" square pan.

Spread date mixture over oat mixture
in the pan.

Pat rest of oat mixture gently but
firmly over dates.

Bake 375 degrees about 30 minutes or
until lightly browned.

Store in refrigerator.

# GINGER DROPS

1 cup sugar
1/2 cup butter
1/2 cup molasses
3 cups flour
1-1/4 tsp cinnamon
1-1/4 tsp ginger
1/2 cup Zucchini milk

1 egg
1 tsp soda
1/2 tsp salt

Cream sugar and butter

Add egg and beat well.

Combine flour, cinnamon, ginger, soda and salt.

Combine molasses and Zucchini milk.

Add molasses mixture and flour mixture alternately to butter mixture.

Mix very well.

Drop on greased cookie sheets.

Bake 350 degrees about 10 minutes.

(Zucchini-milk recipe page 60)

FROST IF DESIRED WITH YOUR FAVORITE GLAZE.

# PINEAPPLE RAISIN COOKIES

1 cup brown sugar, packed     2 cups flour
1/2 cup shortening     1/2 tsp soda
1 tsp baking powder     1/2 tsp salt
1 tsp vanilla     1 egg
1/2 cup raisins     3/4 cup nuts
1/2 cup crushed pineapple, drained
1/2 cup shredded, peeled Zucchini,
    very well drained

Cream sugar, shortening, egg & vanilla.

Add pineapple, zucchini, raisins & nuts.

Mix dry ingredients & add to mixture.

Drop on ungreased sheets & bake 375 degrees about 12 minutes.

Frost if desired with your favorite glaze.

# CARROT COOKIES

1/2 cup shortening     2 cups flour
1/2 cup margarine     1/2 tsp salt
3/4 cup sugar     1/2 tsp cinnamon
1 egg     1/2 cup nuts
2 tsp baking powder     1 tsp vanilla
1-1/2 cups fine ground carrots
3/4 cup shredded, peeled Zucchini,
    Very well drained.

Cream shortening, margarine & sugar.

Beat to fluffy. Add egg and vanilla

Mix dry ingredients & beat into mixture.

Add carrots, zucchini and nuts

Drop on greased sheets and bake 350 degrees about 20 minutes.

Frost if desired with your favorite glaze.

# LEMON CARROT COOKIES

1/2 cup fine grind carrots    1 cup butter
3/4 cup sugar    1 egg
1/2 tsp vanilla    2 cups flour
2 tsp baking powder    1/4 tsp soda
1 cup chopped nuts    1/4 tsp salt
1-1/2 tsp lemon extract
1/2 cup Zucchini, peel, core, grind &
    drain well.

Cream butter and sugar until creamy.

Beat in lemon extract, vanilla, egg, carrots and Zucchini.

Mix together flour, baking powder, salt, and soda.

Add flour mixture to creamed mixture and mix well.

Add nuts.

Drop on greased cookie sheets about 2 inches apart.

Bake 375 degree oven 8 to 10 minutes or until edges are browned.

Frost with your favorite white glaze if desired.

# APPLESAUCE DATE BARS

3/4 cup butter
2 cups flour
1 cup sweet applesauce
1 tsp vanilla
1 cup dates, chopped
1/2 cup white sugar
1/2 cup brown sugar, packed
1 cup Zucchini-sauce, thick

1 egg beaten
2 tsp soda
3 tsp cinnamon
1/2 tsp salt
1 cup nuts, chop

Cream sugars and butter.

Add applesauce and Zucchini-sauce, egg, and vanilla.

Mix flour, cinnamon, salt, soda, nuts, and dates.

Add flour mixture to creamed mixture and mix well.

Bake in greased and floured 9" X 13" pan 350 degrees 25 to 30 minutes to done.

Cool and frost OR serve plain as below.

**FROSTED BARS** Cook 5 tblsp brown sugar, 2 tblsp milk & 2 tblsp butter for one minute.

ADD powder sugar to desired consistency.

**DESSERT** Serve unfrosted, slightly warmed with whip cream or Ice cream.

(Zucchini-sauce recipe page 86)

# PEANUT BUTTER MOLASSES COOKIES

| | |
|---|---|
| 1/3 cup Zucchini milk | 2-1/2 cup flour |
| 3 tblsp evaporated milk | 2 tsp vinegar |
| 3/4 cup peanut butter | 1/2 tsp soda |
| 1/2 cup shortening | 1/2 tsp salt |
| 1 cup packed brown sugar | 1/2 tsp ginger |
| 1/2 tsp cinnamon | 1/2 tsp nutmeg |
| 1/2 cup spanish peanuts | |
| 1/2 cup light molasses | |

Cream peanut butter and shortening until fluffy.

BEAT in brown sugar, molasses, zucchini-milk, evaporated milk and vinegar.

Mix flour, soda, salt, ginger, nutmeg and cinnamon.

Stir flour mixture into creamed mixture and mix well.

Drop on greased cookie sheets.

Press peanuts into tops of cookies and flatten slightly.

Bake 350 degrees 8 to 10 minutes just to lightly brown and firm to touch.

Remove from oven and let set on pans for couple minutes before removing.

Cool on paper towels.

Store in refrigerator.

(Zucchini milk recipe page 60)

# PINEAPPLE BREAD

3 eggs
1 cup salad oil
2 cups sugar
2 tsp vanilla
1/2 tsp baking powder

2 tsp cinnamon
3 cups flour
2 tsp soda
1 tsp salt
1/2 tsp nutmeg

2 cups coarsely shredded Zucchini,
  partly drained.
1 (8 oz) can well drained crushed pineapple
1 cup fine chopped nuts
1 cup fine chopped raisins


Beat eggs to blend. Add oil, sugar and
vanilla.

Beat to thick and foamy.

Stir in Zucchini and pineapple.

Combine flour, soda, salt, baking powder,
cinnamon, nutmeg, nuts and raisins.

Stir into mixture just enough to blend.

Grease and flour 2 loaf pans.

Bake 350 degrees about 1 hour or until
done.

Cool in pans 10 minutes. Turn out on
racks.

Serve slightly warmed slices with butter.


BY: Toni Marie Selander
    Eugene, Oregon

# STRAWBERRY BREAD

1/3 cup cooking oil
1 egg, beaten
3 tsp baking powder
2 cups flour
1/8 tsp allspice
1/2 cup chopped nuts
2/3 cups mashed strawberries
1/2 cup raisins, soaked in hot water for
    5 minutes then very well drained.
1/2 cup shredded, peeled Zucchini,
    well drained.

1/2 tsp soda
1/2 tsp salt
1/2 cup sugar
1 tsp cinnamon
1/2 cup milk

Mix milk, oil and egg together.

Add zucchini, strawberries to milk mixture.

Mix flour, baking powder, allspice, soda, salt, sugar and cinnamon together.

Add nuts and raisins to dry ingredients.

Add dry ingredients to zucchini mixture and stir just to moisten.

Grease & flour a loaf pan and pour mixture into it.

Bake 350 degrees about 50 minute to done.

Cool 20 minutes .

Turn out of pan.

Wait until next day to slice.

Serve slices plain or with butter.

Warm slices slightly in oven if desired.

# PUMPKIN PINEAPPLE BREAD

1/2 cup shortening
3-1/2 cups flour
2 cups canned pumpkin
1/2 tsp baking powder
1 tsp cinnamon

1 cup sugar
4  eggs
1 tsp nutmeg
1 tsp salt
2 tsp soda
1 cup nuts

1 cup Zucchini, chopped very fine
1 cup crushed pineapple in heavy syrup


Melt shortening and beat the eggs.

Add sugar and pumpkin to egg mixture
with the shortening.

Add Zucchini and pineapple with syrup

Mix flour, baking powder, cinnamon,
nutmeg, salt and soda.

Add to creamed mixture and mix.

Add chopped nuts.

Bake in 2 greased 9" loaf pans 350
degrees about 1 hour or until done.


Serve slightly warmed slices with
butter.

Can be warmed under broiler until
butter melts.

# CRANBERRY BREAD

1 cup mayonnaise
1/3 cup orange juice
1-1/2 cups sugar

3 cups flour
1 tsp soda
1 tsp salt

1 cup whole canned cranberry sauce
3/4 cup shredded Zucchini, well drained.
grated rind of one orange
1 cup chopped nuts

Combine cranberries, mayonnaise, Zucchini,
orange juice and rind.

Mix together flour, soda, salt, sugar
and nuts.

Add to cranberry mixture and mix to well
blended.

Line bottoms of 2 small loaf pans with
brown paper and grease lightly.

Pour batter into pans.

Bake 350 degrees about 45 minutes or
until done.

Cool 20 minutes and turn out of pans
onto racks to cool completely.

Serve slices with butter.

# ZUCCHINI SAUCE NUT LOAF

1/2 cup shortening
1 cup Zucchini sauce

1 egg
2 cups flour
1/4 tsp cloves

1 tsp baking powder
1/2 tsp cinnamon
1/2 cup raisins
1/2 tsp nutmeg
2 tblsp apple juice
1-1/4 cup packed brown sugar
1/2 cup chopped nuts

1/2 tsp salt
3/4 tsp soda

Cream shortening and sugar. Add egg.

Mix together flour, baking powder, salt, cinnamon, cloves, soda and nutmeg.

In hot water soak raisins 5 minutes - Drain very well.

Add flour mixture to creamed mixture alternately with Zucchini-sauce and apple juice.

Add raisins and nuts.

Bake in greased 9 X 5" loaf pan about 50 minutes or until done.

Cool and turn out of pan on rack.


## FROSTING

Whip 1 (3 oz) pkg cream cheese with 2 or 3 tblsp milk until smooth.

Spread over loaf.

Serve slices slightly warm

Zucchini sauce recipe-page 86

# RAISIN BREAD

| | |
|---|---|
| 1/2 cup margarine | 1 tsp soda |
| 3/4 cup sugar | 1 tsp salt |
| 2 eggs | 1 tsp cinnamon |
| 1 tsp vanilla | 1/2 tsp nutmeg |
| 2 cups flour | 1/2 cup nuts |
| 1 tsp baking powder | 1/2 cup raisins |

1 cup fine ground Zucchini, undrained.

POUR boiling water over raisins and let set 5 minutes. DRAIN WELL.

Cream margarine and gradually add sugar, beating as you add.

Add eggs and vanilla and mix well.

Combine flour, baking powder, soda, salt, cinnamon, nutmeg, nuts & raisins.

Add to creamed mixture with Zucchini.

Mix only until blended. DO NOT BEAT.

Pour into greased 9" loaf pan and let set 20 minutes.

Bake 350 degrees about 1 hour.

Serve slightly warm slices with butter.

# NUT BREAD

3 eggs
1 cup cooking oil
2 cups sugar
2 tsp vanilla
1/4 tsp baking powder
2 cups grated Zucchini

3 cups flour
1 tsp soda
1 tsp salt
3 tsp cinnamon
1/4 tsp allspice
1/2 cup nuts

Beat eggs to light and foamy.

Add oil, sugar, Zucchini and vanilla.

Mix lightly.

Combine flour, baking powder, soda, salt, cinnamon, allspice and nuts.

Add to oil mixture and stir just to blend.

Grease and flour 2 loaf pans.

Bake 325 degrees about 1 hour to done.

Remove from pans at once and place on racks to cool.

Serve slices plain or with butter.

Warm slices slightly in oven if desired.


BY:
   Vera Kinnaman
   Springfield, Oregon

# CRANBERRY PIE

2 cups cranberries
1 cup Zucchini, peeled & seeds removed
3/4 cup raisins
3 tblsp flour
1-1/4 cup sugar
1 cup water
1 tblsp vanilla


Chop cranberries slightly

Chop the Zucchini fine

Mix the cranberries, Zucchini, raisins, flour, sugar, water and vanilla.

Pour into unbaked 10" pie shell.

Top with unbaked pie shell.

Slit and seal well.

Bake 425 degrees about 40 minutes or until well browned.

Serve as you would a cherry pie.

Best slightly warm with Ice cream.

It is delicious.

# LEMON PIE

1 cup Zucchini milk       1 cup water
4 tblsp cornstarch        1 tblsp butter
1/4 cup lemon juice       6 tblsp honey
2 egg yolks               pinch salt
grated rind of one lemon
1 - 8" pie shell

Heat zucchini milk, water, butter and
honey together.

Combine cornstarch, salt, rind & juice
and add to zucchini mixture.

Cook stirring constantly until thick.

Beat yolks & add a little hot mixture to
them, stir well then add to hot mixture .

Cook 1 minute... Remove from heat.

Pour into baked pie shell & top with
meringue & bake 400 degrees about 5
minutes to brown.. Cool and serve.


## MERINGUE

Beat 2 egg whites until stiff. Add 1
tblsp warmed honey slowly while you
continue to beat.

BY:   MARY MARVIN
      PARTVILLE, N.Y.

("Reprinted by permission of ORGANIC
  GARDENING & FARMING")

     ( ZUCCHINI MILK RECIPE PAGE 60)

# APPLE PIE

3 cups apples, peeled

1-1/2 cups Zucchini, peeled

1-1/2 tsp cinnamon

1/4 tsp nutmeg

1/3 to 1/2 cup sugar

1 to 2 tsp butter


Slice apples thin.

Slice Zucchini thin.

Mix apples, Zucchini, cinnamon, nutmeg, and sugar together.

Pour into unbaked 9" pie shell.

Dot top with butter.

Top with unbaked pie shell.

Seal edges well and slit top.

Bake 350 degrees 45 to 50 minutes until apples and zucchini are tender and top is nicely browned.

Serve the same as you would apple pie.

Slightly warmed with Ice cream is an excellant and delicious way to serve.

# CARROT PIE

1 cup thinly sliced carrots
1 cup Zucchini, peeled and chopped
2/3 cup evaporated milk
1/2 tsp nutmeg
1 tsp cinnamon
1/8 tsp ginger
1/4 tsp salt
2 eggs
1/2 cup sugar
1 cup water
1/4 tsp yellow food coloring
dash salt & dash sugar for cooking

Put carrots, water, dash salt and dash sugar in saucepan and cook 15 minutes.

Add zucchini and continue to cook until vegetables are tender.

Drain and place in blender with food coloring and whirl until pureed. (Or can be beaten with mixer)

In bowl beat eggs lightly; then beat in carrot mixture, milk, 1/2 cup sugar, 1/4 tsp salt, nutmeg, cinnamon, ginger until blended.

Pour into 9" unbaked pie shell.

Bake 375 degrees 45 to 60 minutes or until knife inserted near center comes out clean.

Cool completely.

Serve with whipped cream or Ice cream.

# BUTTERSCOTCH APPLE CREAM PIE

2 cups apples
1 cup Zucchini
1/2 tsp cinnamon
3 tblsp butter
1/4 cup cornstarch
3 egg yolks, slightly beaten
1 cup brown sugar, firmly packed

1/4 cup water
4 tblsp sugar
1/4 tsp salt
2 cups hot milk
1/2 tsp vanilla

Combine peeled, cored, sliced thin apples
and Zucchini in saucepan with water, 4
tblsp sugar and cinnamon.

Cook over low heat until tender and
liquid cooks away.

In another sauce pan combine brown sugar,
salt, cornstarch. Add hot milk slowly
and cook stirring 2 minutes.

Add small amount to egg yolks; then add
yolks to hot mixture.

Cook 1 minute. Remove from heat and add
butter and vanilla.

Cool slightly.

In baked 9" pie shell spread 1/3 of
creamed mixture.

Layer 1/2 of apple mixture; then 1/3 of
creamed mixture, rest of apple mixture
and top with rest of creamed mixture.

Chill.

Serve with whipped cream or Ice cream.

# CHERRY PIE

1/2 tsp red food color
2 tblsp brown sugar
1/4 tsp salt
1 tblsp butter
2 tblsp white sugar
2 tsp lemon juice
1 can water packed red sour cherries
1-1/2 cups cherry juice and water
1 cup shopped, peeled, cored Zucchini
1 pkg (3 oz) vanilla pudding
                    (Not instant )


In saucepan cook Zucchini in the cherry juice and water with 1/4 tsp red food coloring.

Cook until tender in covered kettle.

Add cherries. Bring to boil.

Add combined mixture of pudding, salt, sugars and lemon juice to boiling mixture.

Cook until it comes to full boil.

Add rest of food coloring and the butter.

Stir to melt butter.

Cool slightly.

Pour into 9" graham cracker crust.

CHILL.

SERVE with whipped cream.

# PUMPKIN PIE

2 eggs, slightly beaten
1-1/2 cups pumpkin, cooked & mashed
2/3 cup Zucchini-milk
1 cup evaporated milk or light cream
3/4 cup sugar
1/2 tsp salt
1-1/4 tsp cinnamon
1/2 tsp ginger
1/4 tsp cloves


Mix eggs, pumpkin and Zucchini-milk

Add sugar, salt, cinnamon, ginger & cloves.

Add evaporated milk.

POUR INTO 9" unbaked pie shell.

BAKE 425 degrees 15 minutes.... reduce
temperature to 350 and continue baking
about 40 to 45 minutes or until knife
inserted in center comes out clean.


SERVE cool with whipped cream... Sprinkle
a few chopped nuts or coconut over whip
cream.


NOTE: If your pie pans are small 9" use
      10" instead.. This makes a lot
      of filling.



(Zucchini-milk recipe page 60)

# APPLESAUCE PIE

1/3 cup light corn syrup     2 eggs
1/2 cup applesauce           1/2 cup sugar
1 tsp cinnamon               1/3 cup milk
1 tblsp margarine            1/4 tsp salt
1 tsp vanilla                1/4 cup nuts
1 tblsp lemon juice
2/3 cup Zucchini, peeled and chopped
  fine with seeds removed.

2 tblsp chopped raisins

1-1/4 cup bran flakes


Combine syrup and sugar in sauce pan and
bring to boil.

In bowl beat eggs and slowly add syrup
beating as added.

Mix in margarine.

Add applesauce, cinnamon, vanilla, lemon
juice, milk, salt, nuts, raisins and
Zucchini.

Stir in bran flakes.

Pour into 9" unbaked pie shell.

Bake 375 degrees about 40 to 50 minutes
until knife inserted in center comes
out clean.

Serve with whip cream or Ice cream.

# PINEAPPLE CHEESECAKE PIE

8 oz cream cheese, beat to soft
2 cups cold milk
2 tblsp sugar, (for pudding mixture)
1/2 tsp vanilla
1 pkg instant lemon pudding mix
2 cups crushed pineapple with juice
3 tblsp cornstarch
1/4 cup sugar
1-1/4 tsp lemon extract
1/4 cup water
1 cup Zucchini, peeled, seeded and chopped fine

In kettle: Mix Zucchini and 1/4 cup pineapple juice from the pineapple.

Cook until zucchini is tender about 15 to 20 minutes on low heat. Drain.

Add pineapple with juice, water, sugar, and cornstarch and cook over low heat until thickened.. Set aside to cool.


IN BOWL:

Beat cheese and blend in 1/2 cup milk; then add rest of milk, the 2 tblsp sugar, pudding mix, vanilla & lemon.

Beat 2 minutes. Pour into graham cracker crust. Chill.

Spoon pineapple mixture over pudding and chill in refrigerator.

# GLAZED APPLE PIE

3/4 cup sugar
2 cups Zucchini
3 cups apples
1/4 tsp nutmeg
1 tsp cinnamon
2 tblsp orange juice

3 tblsp flour
1/8 tsp salt
1/2 cup raisins
3 tblsp butter

Peel & remove the seeds from Zucchini
and chop or slice thin.

Peel and core apples and slice thin.

Mix sugar, flour, cinnamon, salt, nutmeg.

Mix in the apples, Zucchini and raisins.

Pour into 9" unbaked pie shell: Sprinkle
with orange juice and dot with butter.

Top with unbaked shell; Seal and slit.

Bake 400 degrees 40 minutes or until
apples and Zucchini are tender.

Drizzle with glaze. (Recipe below)

## GLAZE

MIX together: 1 cup powder sugar,
              1 tsp grated orange rind
              3 tblsp orange juice

Beat until smooth.

Drizzle over hot pie.

# PINEAPPLE PIE

3/4 cup sugar          1 cup milk
2 tblsp cornstarch     dash of salt
3 egg yolks, beaten    3 egg whites
1/2 cup Zucchini, chopped fine
1 cup crushed pineapple, Drain and
reserve juice.


Peel and remove seeds from Zucchini.
Chop into small pieces.

Cook in pineapple juice until tender.

Mix sugar, cornstarch, & salt together.

Add milk and egg yolks.

Mix in pineapple.

Drain cooked Zucchini and mix in with
pineapple mixture.

Beat egg whites and fold in mixing
for several minutes.

Pour into 9" unbaked pie shell.

Bake 350 degrees 45 to 60 minutes or
until knife inserted in center comes
out clean.

CHILL BEFORE SERVING.

# APPLE CRUMB DESSERT

3/4 cup packed brown sugar  
3/4 cup butter  
1-1/3 cup flour  
3/4 tsp baking powder  
1 tsp cinnamon  
1/2 cup crushed Wheat Chex cereal  
1 cup pared thin sliced apples  
1 cup pared thin sliced Zucchini  

1 egg  
1 tsp vanilla  
1/3 cup milk  
1/2 tsp salt  

Cream butter and sugar; Add egg and vanilla and blend well.

Mix together the dry ingredients.

Add to creamed mixture; Blend well.

Stir in milk and chex and mix well.

Spread 1/2 of batter in greased 9" pan.

Layer 1/2 apple slices and 1/2 zucchini slices over batter.

Sprinkle with 1/2 of crumb topping.

Repeat with batter, apple, zucchini and topping.

Bake 375 degrees about 40 minutes or until apples & zucchini are tender.

Serve warm with Ice cream or whip cream.

## CRUMB TOPPING

Combine 1/2 cup flour, 1/4 cup sugar, 1/4 cup packed brown sugar and 3/4 tsp cinnamon.

Cut in 1/4 cup butter until coarse and crumbly.

Add 1/3 cup chopped nuts

# BREAD PUDDING

2 cups Zucchini milk      1/4 tsp salt
1/2 tsp cinnamon          2 tblsp butter
1/4 cup honey             1 tsp vanilla
1/2 cup raisins
1-1/2 cup cubed bread crusts
2 eggs, slightly beaten

Bring Zucchini milk to boiling point.

Pour over bread cubes. Add butter.

Combine honey, salt & eggs. Add to bread mixture. Add rest of ingredients.

Pour into greased casserole dish. Set dish in shallow pan of hot water & bake 350 degrees for about 1 hour.


## HOW TO MAKE ZUCCHINI MILK

Peel Zucchini, but do not remove seeds or pulp.. CUT into chunks about 1" in size and put in blender, filling about 1/4 or less.

Switch to liquefy and let run until it becomes a liquid.

Measure liquid for recipes.

Can be frozen for later use if desired.

RECIPE & ZUCCHINI MILK IDEA BY:
    MARY MARVIN, PARTVILLE, N.Y.

("reprinted by permission of ORGANIC
  GARDENING & FARMING")

# APPLE SQUARES

2 cups Zucchini, Peeled & sliced thin
4 cups apples, Peeled & sliced thin
1 cup white sugar
1/4 cup packed brown sugar
1/8 tsp salt
2 tsp cinnamon

Combine all above ingredients. SET ASIDE.

# CRUST

2-1/2 cups flour        1/2 tsp salt
2 tsp brown sugar       1 cup shortening
2 egg whites            2 egg yolks
milk

Mix flour, sugar & salt - ADD shortening
and mix with fork until crumbly.

Place yolks in measuring cup and add
milk to equal 2/3 cup.. Mix together.

Add milk to flour and mix until dough
forms a ball.

Place on slight  floured board and roll
1/2 at a time to fit 9 X 13" pan.

Place bottom crust in greased pan.

Spread apple mixture on dough. Top with
rest of crust.

Beat  egg whites to frothy, Spread on top.

Bake 400 degrees for about 40 minutes or
until apples & zucchini are done.

Serve warm or cold with whip topping.

# APPLE PUDDING

| | |
|---|---|
| 1 cup sugar | 1 tsp soda |
| 1/4 cup butter | 1/4 tsp salt |
| 2 cups apples | 1/2 tsp nutmeg |
| 1 cup Zucchini | 1 cup flour |
| 1-3/4 tsp cinnamon | 1 tsp vanilla |
| 1/2 cup nuts | 1 egg |

Cream sugar and butter.. Add egg and vanilla and beat well.

Combine flour, and spices. Then add to creamed mixture.

Add peeled and very fine chopped apples and zucchini.

Add chopped nuts.  STIR WELL.

BAKE in greased 9" pyrex baking dish 300 degrees about 1 hour or until apples and zucchini are done.

SERVE warm with warm sauce and whip cream or Ice cream.


## SAUCE

| | |
|---|---|
| 1/2 cup packed brown sugar | 1/2 cup butter |
| | 1 tsp vanilla |
| 1/2 cup white sugar | 1/4 tsp cinnamon |
| 1 cup half & half milk | |

Combine all ingredients and cook over low heat for about 5 minutes...

STIR constantly.. POUR warm over pudding when served.

# APPLE MAPLE PUDDING

2 cups apples           1 tblsp flour
1 cup Zucchini          1/4 tsp salt
1/3 cup maple syrup     2 tblsp water
3/4 tsp cinnamon

Peel and slice thin apples & Zucchini.

Mix all ingredients & place in deep
greased baking dish.

Bake 400 degrees 30 minutes covered.

Reduce heat to 350 degrees.. Spread
following topping over and continue
baking 30 minutes uncovered until top
is done.

## TOPPING

2 tblsp shortening      1/2 cup  sugar
2 tsp baking powder     1 egg
1/2 tsp salt            1 cup flour
1/2 cup milk

Cream shortening and sugar. ADD egg.

Mix flour, baking powder and salt.

Add alternately with milk to creamed
mixture.

Pour over apple & zucchini mixture and
spread even to edges.

Follow baking instructions above.


Serve slightly warm with cream or Ice
cream.

# APPLE CRISP

3 to 4 cups baking apples,
   Peeled and chopped

1-1/2 cups Zucchini,
   Peel, remove seeds & chop fine.

3/4 cup butter
1 cup packed brown sugar
1-1/2 cups quick oatmeal
3/4 cup flour
3 tsp cinnamon


Mix apples and zucchini in bottom of
well buttered baking dish.

Melt butter and stir in the sugar,
flour, oatmeal and cinnamon.

MIX WELL.

Spread over apples and zucchini.

Bake 350 degrees about 45 minutes or
until apples and zucchini are tender.

SERVE warm with cream or Ice cream.

# APPLE DESSERT

3 cups apples
1 cup Zucchini
1/3 cup brown sugar
1 tblsp butter
1 tsp cinnamon
1 tsp baking powder
1/8 tsp butter flavor
1 tsp almond flavoring

1/2 cup sugar
1 tblsp butter
1 egg, beaten
1/2 cup flour
1/8 tsp nutmeg
1/2 tsp vanilla

Peel, core and slice apples and Zucchini
into buttered 9" pyrex baking dish.

Combine packed brown sugar, 1 tblsp butter,
cinnamon, nutmeg and butter flavoring.

Sprinkle over apples and zucchini.

Cream together white sugar, butter & egg.

Mix flour and baking powder together.

Stir almond and vanilla flavoring into
creamed mixture.

Add flour and stir to well mixed.

Spread over apples. (this will be a
thin layer)

Bake 350 degrees for about 30 minutes
on middle rack until Zucchini and
apples are tender.

Serve slightly warm with cream or
Ice cream.

# APPLESAUCE BREAD PUDDING

1/4 cup brown sugar
1 cup applesauce
1 cup Zucchini-sauce
2 tsp lemon juice

4 tblsp butter
3 egg yolks
1 tsp cinnamon
1/8 tsp nutmeg

1/2 tsp grated lemon rind
2 cups diced, whole wheat bread

Melt butter to sizzling... ADD bread
and saute to brown & slightly crisp.

Beat yolks, add applesauce, zucchini-
sauce, sugar, cinnamon, nutmeg, juice
and rind.. FOLD in bread and pour into
greased casserole dish.

Bake 350 degrees 35 minutes uncovered
until lightly brown on top.

Top with meringue and bake  few minutes
until browned.


## MERINGUE

BEAT 3 egg whites, 1/8 tsp salt until
stiff... ADD 6 tblsp sugar, one at a
time beating after each... ADD 1/2 tsp
lemon extract.. Beat to stiff.

Spread over top of pudding.. Bake until
brown.

Serve slightly warm with cream.


(ZUCCHINI-SAUCE RECIPE PAGE 86)

# APPLE BREAD PUDDING

3/4 cup Zucchini      1 cup milk
3/4 cup apples       1/4 cup flour
1/3 cup sugar        1/4 tsp cloves
3/4 cup raisins      3 eggs
1/4 tsp nutmeg       1 tsp cinnamon

2 cups coarse stale bread crusts, cubed.

Mix bread, with the milk and cook until
it absorbs the milk.

Peel and remove seeds from Zucchini
and apples and chop fine.

Mix Zucchini, apples, sugar, raisins,
flour, beaten eggs, cinnamon, cloves
and nutmeg.

Add to bread & milk mixture.

Stir well.

Pour into heavy buttered baking dish.

BAKE 375 degrees about 45 minutes or
until knife inserted in center comes
out clean.

SERVE WARM WITH CREAM.

# CRANBERRY PUDDING

3/4 cup light molasses    1 cup Zucchini
1/2 cup boiling water    2 cups cranberries
2-1/4 cups flour    1/2 cup raisins
1 cup chopped walnuts    3 tsp soda

Wash raw cranberries - Peel, remove seeds and chop fine the Zucchini.

Put cranberries, zucchini & raisins in a bowl. Add molasses and boiling water.

Mix flour & soda and add to cranberry mixture.

Add nuts.

Stir to blend.

Pour into greased & lightly sugared 9 X 13" pan. Cover top of pan lightly with foil.

Bake 325 degree oven about 1 hour.

Serve warm with hot sauce below.


HOT SAUCE


COMBINE: 2 cups   sugar, 1/2 cup butter, 1 cup light cream in pan.

Bring to boil & cook 3 minutes stir constantly. Remove from heat and add 2 tsp vanilla.

Serve hot over warm pudding squares.

# GREEN TOMATO PUDDING

1-1/2 cup green tomatoes
1 cup zucchini
1/4 cup water
3 tblsp white sugar
1/4 cup packed brown sugar
1 tblsp butter

1/3 cup raisins
1 tsp cinnamon
1/8 tsp salt
4 tsp flour

Peel and slice thin the zucchini - Slice the tomatoes thin.

In deep casserole mix all ingredients and put in oven and bake covered 25 minutes at 400 degrees.

## TOPPING

1/2 cup sugar
2 tblsp shortening
2 tsp baking powder
1/2 cup milk

1 egg
1 cup flour
1/2 tsp salt

Cream shortening and sugar.

Add egg and mix well.

Mix flour, baking powder and salt.

Add alternately with milk to creamed mixture.    MIX WELL.

Pour over tomato mixture in casserole and return to oven and bake 350 degrees about 30 to 40 minutes until top is done.

Serve warm with whip cream or Ice cream.

# CHERRY COBBLER

1-1/2 cups flour
1-1/2 tsp baking powder
1/4 tsp salt
1/4 cup shortening
1/4 cup milk
1 cup Zucchini
2 cups Red sour cherries, drained

1 egg
1 tblsp sugar
1/2 cup sugar
Red coloring

Peel and remove seeds from Zucchini; chop very fine.

Drain cherries and mash.

Mix Zucchini, cherries, 1/2 cup sugar and red food coloring to tint.

Place in greased 8" X 8" baking pan.

Mix flour, baking powder, salt and 1 tblsp sugar.

Cut in shortening. Add egg and milk, which have been beaten together and mix to form dough.

Turn out on floured board and knead lightly to blend.

Pat out to fit the baking pan and place on top of cherries.

Bake 400 degrees 25 minutes or until crust is brown.

Serve warm with cream or Ice cream.

# BASIC DOUGH FOR ROLLS

1 cup whole milk
1/2 cup evaporated milk
1/2 cup Zucchini-milk
1/2 cup shortening
3 tsp dry yeast
1/4 cup warm water

2-1/4 tsp salt
1/4 cup sugar
6 cups flour
3 egg yolks
dash sugar

Scald whole and evaporated milk.

Add shortening, salt, & sugar. STIR TO melt shortening and dissolve sugar.

Cool to lukewarm.

Dissolve yeast in warm water & dash sugar.

To cooled milk add the Zucchini-milk & stir.. Add 1 cup flour and beat with beater.. Add eggs & yeast and beat.

Continue to add flour little at a time beating with beater as long as you can. Then work in rest of flour with large spoon.

Let dough rise in warm place to double.

Pat out on floured board and cut into 2" squares. Stretch each slightly & drop filling (From page 72) in center..

Bring up corners and seal well.

Place upside down in greased muffin tins and let rise..

Bake 350 degrees 20 minutes.

Remove from pans and brush tops with melted butter.

  (Zucchini-milk recipe page 60)

# FILLINGS FOR ROLLS

## PRUNE

MIX TOGETHER: 1 cup cooked, pitted, mashed prunes, 1/2 cup sugar, 2 tblsp prune juice, 1/2 tsp cinnamon and 1/2 tsp grated lemon rind.

## APPLE

IN SAUCEPAN mix 4 cups peeled, chopped apples, 3/4 cup sugar, 1/4 cup water, 1 tblsp lemon juice, 1/2 tsp grated lemon rind and 1/4 tsp cinnamon. COOK until apples are done.

## POPPY SEED

| | |
|---|---|
| 1-1/4 cup milk | 1 egg |
| 1/2 tsp cinnamon | 1 tsp vanilla |
| 2 tblsp honey | 2 tblsp butter |
| 2/3 cup sugar | |
| 1/2 tsp grated lemon rind | |
| 2 cups ground poppy seeds. | |

(Measure lightly - Do not pack)

SIMMER poppy seed in milk for 5 minutes.

Add sugar, butter, vanilla, cinnamon, and lemon rind. SIMMER 5 minutes.

BLEND in honey, & cool to room temp.

BLEND in slightly beaten egg yolk & fold in stiff beaten egg white.

(DOUGH RECIPE PAGE 71)

# APPLE FILLED ROLLS

1-1/2 cups milk    2 tsp salt
1/2 cup cream    1/4 cup sugar
1/2 cup shortening   6 cups flour
1 sq. compressed yeast
1/4 cup water, lukewarm
4 egg yolks

Scald milk & cream; Add salt, sugar & shortening. Cool to lukewarm.

Dissolve yeast in water.

With electric mixer beat into milk 1 cup flour, then the egg yolks & yeast.

Beat in up to about 5 cups of flour, use mixer as long as possible, then work with spoon until all flour is mixed in.

Place in greased large bowl and let rise in warm place until doubled.

Pat out on floured board and cut into 2" squares, stretch each slightly.

Drop filling in centers & bring up the corners & seal. Place upside down in greased muffin pans. Let rise to double.

Bake 350 degreees about 20 minutes.

Remove from pans to cool.

## FILLING

Cook 2-1/2 cups peeled chopped apples, 1-1/2 cup peeled, seeded chopped Zucchini, 2/3 cup sugar, 1/4 cup apple juice, 1-1/2 tsp cinnamon until tender.

Drain and mash lightly. Fill rolls as directed in recipe above.

# CINNAMON ROLLS

FOLLOW BASIC DOUGH FOR ROLLS PAGE 71.

After dough rises first time; Pat dough
out on floured board in rectangler shape.

Spread with butter; Sprinkle with brown
sugar; then with cinnamon and raisins
as desired.

Roll up as you would a jelly roll; Seal
edges well.

With sharp knife cut 1/2" slices and
place in greased muffin tins.

Let rise to double.

Bake 350 degrees about 20 minutes.

Brush with butter and remove from pans
onto rack to cool.

Frost with your favorite white glaze.

Serve warm with butter.

# NUT ROLL

Use basic dough recipe page 71- After
first rise pat out on floured board
into a rectangle.

Mix 1/4 cup butter, 3/4 cup brown sugar,
1/2 cup chopped nuts & 1 tsp cinnamon.

Spread on dough and roll dough up like
jelly roll; Place in greased tube pan
and let rise to double in warm place.

Bake 350 degrees 30 minutes to done.

Turn out of pan immediately onto rack.

Serve slices with butter.

# PINEAPPLE MARMALADE

1/4 cup pineapple juice
4 cups Zucchini, peeled
5 tblsp lemon juice
1-1/2 stick cinnamon
2 large oranges
4 cups sugar
1 pkg pectin (1-3/4 oz)
1 cup unsweetened crushed pineapple, drained.

Grind medium coarsely the Zucchini and seeded oranges with rind.

Add pineapple and juices and cinnamon.

Bring to boil and simmer slowly until Zucchini is tender about 20 minutes uncovered.

Add pectin and bring to boil. Add sugar and boil hard for 1 minute stirring constantly.

Seal in jars... Makes about 2 pints.


VARIATION

FOLLOW the above recipe and add slivered rind of 1/2 lemon and 1 tsp fine chopped candied ginger to the first cooking.

Add pectin and bring to boil. Add sugar and boil hard for 1 minute stirring constantly.

Seal in jars.

# APPLE PEAR JAM

| | |
|---|---|
| 1 cup pears | 1 cup apples |
| 1 cup zucchini | 3/4 cup sugar |
| 1 tblsp lemon juice | 1 tsp cinnamon |

Peel and remove seeds from pears and apples and chop fine.

Peel zucchini and chop fine.

In saucepan place pears, apples, zucchini and sugar.

Cook on low heat until thickened.

Add cinnamon and lemon juice

Mash to desired consistency.

Seal in sterile jars.

## NOTE

If you prefer to use pectin in cooking you may,but be sure to cook long enough for fruit and zucchini to get tender.

Follow cooking instructions on pectin package.

# CANTALOUPE MARMALADE

3 cups cantaloupe
3 cups Zucchini
2 cups crushed pineapple with juice
4 tsp lemon juice
6 cups sugar
2 oranges
4 - 2" sticks of cinnamon


Core and peel cantaloupe. Chop in pieces.

Peel and chop Zucchini into pieces.

In separate kettles cook cantaloupe and zucchini in water until tender.

Drain both and mash very well.

Combine sugar, lemon juice, pineapple with juice, and add mashed cantaloupe and Zucchini.

Slice oranges very thin, then chop fine.

Add oranges and cinnamon sticks to kettle.

Cook slowly for about 30 minutes or until thickened.

Stir often

Pour into hot sterile jars and seal.

# CARROT PINEAPPLE MARMALADE

1-1/2 cups carrots    1/4 cup lemon
1-1/3 cups Zucchini     rind, shredded
6 cinnamon sticks
1/4 cup lemon juice    3 cups sugar
2 cups crushed pineapple, well drained.


In separate kettles cook the peeled
carrots and Zucchini to tender. Drain and
mash.

In large saucepan combine carrots, lemon
rind, zucchini, lemon juice, pineapple
with juice  and cinnamon sticks.

Bring to boil and simmer slowly for
10 minutes.

Add sugar and bring to boil.

Reduce heat and simmer slowly for about
30 minutes or until thick. Stir often to
avoid scorching.

Ladle into hot sterile jars and seal.

Process 10 minutes in simmering water
bath (185 degrees)

Remove from water and set aside to cool
and seal.

NOTE: Add 1/2 cup sugar for a sweeter
      marmalade.

      Put pineapple through blender
      for a smoother marmalade.

# STRAWBERRY JAM

2 cups strawberries, unsweetened frozen
1-1/2 cups Zucchini
1-1/4 cup sugar
1 tsp cinnamon
1 tblsp lemon juice


Peel and chop fine the Zucchini.

In saucepan put strawberries, Zucchini, sugar, cinnamon, and lemon juice.

Cook over low heat until thick about 30 minutes.

Stir often to prevent burning.

Mash to make a smoother jam.


Seal in sterile jars.


## NOTE

If you prefer to use pectin in cooking you may do so. But be sure to cook long enough for Zucchini to get tender.

FOLLOW cooking instructions on pectin package for strawberry jam.

# TOMATO SALAD

COMBINE: 1/4 cup relish - 1 tblsp white
vinegar - 1/2 tsp sugar and
1/4 tsp salt.

ADD: 1-1/2 cup fine chopped Zucchini
and 1 small cut up tomato.

CHILL & SERVE ON LETTUCE LEAVES.

# TOMATO ONION SALAD

2 cups fine chopped Zucchini
2 small tomato, cut up
3 tblsp chopped green onion
2 tblsp chopped fresh parsley
5 tblsp salad oil
2/3 cup white vinegar
1/2 to 3/4 tsp salt
1/8 tsp pepper

COMBINE oil, vinegar, salt & pepper. MIX
vegetables and pour oil mixture over.
TOSS & CHILL several hours, stirring
once in awhile. SERVE on lettuce leaves.

# TUNA SALAD

MIX: 1/3 cup mayonnaise - 2 tsp
chopped pickle & 1/2 tsp celery seed.

ADD: 1/2 cup coarse shredded Zucchini -
1/2 cup shredded carrots & 1/3 cup
tuna, drained. TOSS lightly & CHILL.

SERVE on lettuce leaves with tomato
pieces.

# LIME JELLO SALAD

1 pkg (3 oz) Lime Jell-o   3/4 tsp salt
1 cup boiling water   2 tblsp vinegar
3/4 cup cold water   1/2 cup cabbage
1 tsp grated onion   1/2 cup carrots
1/4 cup celery
1 tblsp green pepper
1 cup Zucchini, peeled & seeds removed


Dissolve jell-o in boiling water.

Add salt and stir to dissolved.

Add cold water, vinegar and onion.

Chill to thickened slightly.

Chop fine, the celery, green pepper and cabbage.

Shred the raw carrots and Zucchini & add all ingredients together. Then pour into 3 or 4 cup mold.

Chill to firm.

Unmold and garnish with green parsley and lettuce and tomatoes.

# HOTDOG & HAMBURGER RELISH

3 cups unpeeled Zucchini
1/2 cup chopped onion
3-1/2 tsp pickling salt
2 tblsp chopped green pepper
1 tblsp chopped red pepper
8 tblsp white vinegar
1/4 tsp dry mustard

1 cup sugar
1/4 tsp nutmeg
1-1/2 tsp celery seed

Grind coarsely the zucchini; Add onion & salt and let stand overnight. IN MORNING place in colander to drain.

Add rest of ingredients to zucchini and cook very slow about 20 minutes

Stir often.. SEAL in jars.

# SLICED PICKLES

8 cups zucchini
1-1/2 cup onion
4 tblsp pickle salt
2-1/4 cup white vinegar
3 tsp mustard seed
3/4 tsp turmeric

2-1/2 cup sugar
1 tsp cloves
1/2 tsp celery seed

Slice unpeeled zucchini; Slice onion; Add salt & 2 trays of ice. LET SET for about 3 hours. Rinse off part of salt.

Mix rest of ingredients & bring to boil.

Add zucchini & onion which have been well drained. Bring mixture to boil and cook about 1 minute.

Seal in jars

# WATERMELON RIND PICKLES

8 cups Zucchini, cored.      8 cups sugar
10 cups watermelon rind      2 lemons
16 cups water                4 cups vinegar
1 cup salt                   2 cups water
cloves                       allspice
stick cinnamon


Pare melon & zucchini. Cut into 1" cubes
in separate bowls.

Combine 16 cups water & 1 cup salt..Pour
over cubes.. Refrigerate overnight.

IN MORNING: Drain melon rind & place in
large kettle & cover with fresh water.
Bring to boiling & simmer to tender.

Drain Zucchini and add to melon & bring
to boil... Simmer 5 minutes.. DRAIN

Combine sugar, thin sliced lemons, 2 tblsp
whole cloves, 2 tblsp whole allspice, 8"
of cinnamon stick, vinegar, 2 cups water
and bring to boil.

Add melon rinds and zucchini and simmer
until zucchini is tender about 20
minutes and rinds are clear.

Pour into hot sterile jars and seal.

Ready in 3 to 5 days.


THESE ARE A QUITE SWEET PICKLE.

(If desired you can cut down on the
sugar for a not so sweet pickle)

# CABBAGE SLAW

1/4 cup salad oil
1/4 cup vinegar
1/4 tsp celery seed
1/2 cup sugar
1/4 tsp salt
2 cups shredded cabbage
1-1/2 cups peeled, cored, Zucchini.


Mix salad oil, vinegar, sugar, salt, and celery salt together in saucepan.

Bring to boil and simmer covered for about 1 minute.

Shred cabbage and zucchini into a large bowl.

Pour boiling syrup over and stir to mix well.

Chill and refrigerate before serving.

This will keep nicely for several days in refrigerator.

If desired 1/2 cup shredded carrots may be add to cabbage and zucchini.

# SWEET & SOUR TOMATO MARMALADE

1 cup Zucchini

1/3 cup cider vinegar

1 cup sugar

1 tsp salt

1 tsp mixed pickling spices

3 cups red tomatoes


Scald tomatoes, remove skins and cut into small pieces.

Peel zucchini and chop very fine.

In saucepan combine vinegar, sugar, salt and spices.

Add tomatoes and zucchini.

Bring to boil and cook over low heat until it begins to thicken.

Stir often; it takes about 20 to 30 minutes.

Seal in sterile jars.

Serve as a relish with roast, ham or pork chops.

# PUMPKIN PANCAKES

1/4 cup melted shortening   2 cups flour
1/2 cup canned pumpkin    1 tsp salt
1-1/2 cups milk         1/4 tsp nutmeg
4 tsp baking powder      3 eggs
1-1/2 tsp cinnamon
1/2 cup Zucchini-sauce (Recipe below)

Beat eggs; Add milk, shortening, pumpkin, & Zucchini. Mix dry ingredients and add.

Bake on hot greased griddle. Turn once.

WAFFLES: Make a thinner batter by adding more milk. Separate egg & beat whites & fold into batter. Bake on hot waffle iron.

# CINNAMON PANCAKES

1 cup Bisquick baking mix
1 egg
1/2 cup Zucchini-sauce
2 or 3 tblsp milk
1-1/2 tsp cinnamon
1/2 tsp lemon juice

Beat all together and bake on hot greased griddle or fry pan.

### ZUCCHINI-SAUCE

Peel 3 cups Zucchini. Chop up in sauce pan with 1/2 cup apple juice and dash salt. Cook until tender.

Drain well and mash.

Makes 1 cup Zucchini-sauce. (Freezes well)

86

# ZUCCHINI CASSEROLE

6 cups sliced Zucchini       1 cup carrots
1 cup dairy sour cream       1/4 cup onion
1/2 cup margarine, melted
1 can condensed cream of chicken soup
1 (8 oz) pkg. Herb-seasoned stuffing mix.

Cook Zucchini and onion in salted water for 5 minutes. DRAIN.

Combine soup and sour cream. Shred raw carrots and stir in.

Fold in Zucchini and chopped onion.

Combine stuffing mix and margarine.

Spread 1/2 of stuffing in 12 X 7 X 2" baking dish.

Spoon mixture on top; Then spread with rest  of stuffing over all.

Bake 350 degrees about 25 minutes.

**BY**: June Shelby
      Eugene, Oregon

# STUFFED ZUCCHINI

Mix 1/2 lb sausage with 1/4 cup raw rice.

Hollow out Zucchini. Place in baking dish and stuff mixture in hollow. Pour 1/2 cup mushroom soup on top.

Bake 350 degrees about 45 minutes or until sausage is done & Zucchini tender.

# CHEESY BURGER CASSEROLE

4 or 5 small Zucchini (about 2 lbs)
1-1/4 lb hamburger
1/2 cup chopped onion
1/4 cup green pepper chopped
1 tsp salt
1/8 tsp pepper
3/4 cup Velvetta cheese - diced
1 can mushroom soup
1/2 cup bread crumbs
2 tblsp butter , melted


Wash zucchini - Do not peel - Cut into slices and cook in boiling water for about 4 minutes; Drain well.

Brown hamburger, onion and green pepper in fry pan; Drain off grease.

Layer meat, zucchini and cheese in 2 quart greased baking dish, Sprinkle salt & pepper over each layer of meat and zucchini.

Spread soup over top and bake 350 degrees 30 minutes.

Mix melted butter with bread crumbs and sprinkle over top of casserole. Return to oven 15 minutes more.


NOTE: Cheese may be increased or decreased according to individual taste.

# MEATLOAF

1-1/2 lbs ground beef
1/4 cup chopped onion
3 tblsp catsup
2 tblsp brown sugar
1 cup soft stale bread crumbs
1/2 cup coarse ground Zucchini
1 tsp worcestershire sauce

2 eggs
1 tsp salt
1/4 tsp pepper

Mix beef, crumbs, onion, eggs, zucchini, salt, pepper & worcestershire sauce.

Place in loaf pan. Dribble catsup over top and sprinkle with brown sugar.

Bake 350 degrees about 60 minutes.

Baste occasionally with drippings.

# MEATBALLS

2 slices bread
1 tblsp chopped onion
1 cup tomato juice
1 lb ground lean beef
1/2 cup Zucchini, Ground & well drained.

1 egg
1/2 tsp salt
1/8 tsp pepper

Moisten bread with some water & squeeze out well. Crumble into bowl & add beef, egg, onion, salt, pepper & Zucchini.

Shape into small balls & brown on both sides in fry pan. Drain off fat.

Pour tomato juice over; cover & simmer about 15 minutes. Uncover & simmer until sauce is slightly thickened.

# BAKED FILLED ZUCCHINI

1 tblsp margarine
3 Zucchini (2" thick)
1 cup ground beef
1 (8 oz) can tomato sauce
1/4 cup grated parmesan cheese
2 tblsp onion
1/4 cup celery
salt and pepper


Cook Zucchini in boiling salted water for about 3 minutes.

Cut in half lengthwise.

Scoop out pulp and salt and pepper it to taste.

Melt margarine in fry pan; Add chopped celery and ground beef. Cook to lightly browned. Drain off fat.

Add pulp and tomato sauce.

Stuff mixture in Zucchini hollows.

Place in shallow baking pan and sprinkle with the parmesan cheese.

Bake 375 degrees about 30 minutes or until nice and tender.

Serve piping hot with salad.

# CHICKEN STEW

2 cups sliced Zucchini
2 lb chicken, cut up
1 can cream of celery soup
1 tsp paprika (optional)
1/2 cup drained, chopped canned tomatoes.
1/2 cup cooked, sliced carrots
2 tblsp onion, chopped
1/4 cup water
1/2 tsp crushed basil leaves
1 clove garlic (optional)
1/2 cup canned small potatoes, sliced


Roll chicken in flour; Sprinkle lightly
with salt and pepper.

Brown in hot fat in skillet on both
sides.

DRAIN OFF FAT.

Add soup, water, paprika, basil leaves
and garlic and onion.

Cover and simmer 30 minutes stirring
often.

Add Zucchini and tomato.

Cook 10 minutes.

Add carrots and potatoes.

Heat thoroughly.

Serve over cooked noodles or rice.

ORIGINAL RECIPE DONATED BY:  Gerry Ware
           Harrisburg, Oregon

# SKILLET MACARONI

| | |
|---|---|
| 1 lb ground beef | 1 tsp sugar |
| 1/4 cup chopped onion | 2 cups hot water |
| 1 can (1 lb) tomatoes | salt & pepper |
| 1 cup macaroni (uncooked) | |

Cut tomatoes to bite size.

Peel, seed and chop into small pieces
1 cup Zucchini.

Brown beef and onion in fry pan. DRAIN.

Stir in hot water.. ADD salt and pepper
to taste.

Add tomatoes, sugar, Zucchini and
uncooked elbow macaroni.

Simmer slowly about 20 to 30 minutes.

Stir occasionally & cook until macaroni
is tender.

NOTE: If it seems to get dry before
done, just add more tomato juice
or a little water.


IF DESIRED - uncooked noodles may be
used in place of macaroni.

ADD about 2 cups uncooked and decrease
the cooking time.

# CHICKEN & ZUCCHINI

2 tblsp cooking oil
2-1/2 lbs frying chicken
1/2 cup onion, chopped
1 (11 oz) can cream of celery soup
4 tsp worcestershire sauce
1/2 tsp salt
1/2 tsp oregano leaves, crumbled
2 cups zucchini, unpeeled & sliced
1 small can green beans, drained


In fry pan brown chicken in the oil.

Add onions & saute to tender.

Stir in soup, worcestershire sauce, salt,
oregano and bring to boiling.

Cover and simmer slowly until chicken
is done, about 30 to 45 minutes.

Add zucchini and simmer to tender.

Add beans and heat through.

Serve piping hot with biscuits

# SALMON & ZUCCHINI DISH

1-2/3 cup shredded, peeled Zucchini
4 tblsp onion, fine chopped
3 eggs, beaten
1/3 to 1/2 cup grated parmesan cheese
3 tsp lemon juice
4 tblsp fresh parsley, snipped
1/4 tsp salt
dash of pepper
1 -8 oz can red salmon, drain, remove
   the cartilage and flake.


In pan, combine zucchini and onion; Add
enough water to cover; Bring to boil and
simmer covered to just tender.

Drain well and squeeze out excess liquid.

Combine eggs, cheese and lemon juice; Add
to zucchini mixture.

Add parsley, salt and pepper.

Fold in salmon and turn into ungreased
8 inch pie plate.

Bake 350 degrees until set about 25 to
30 minutes.

Serve hot with crackers.

# ZUCCHINI NOODLE CASSEROLE

4 cups zucchini, diced
3/4 to 1 cup shredded swiss cheese
3 cups uncooked fine noodles
1 (10-3/4 oz) can vegetarian vegetable soup
1 soup-can of water
2 tsp worcestershire sauce
1/2 tsp salt
1/2 tsp oregano


Mix together zucchini, noodles, soup,
water, 1/2 of the cheese, worcestershire,
salt and oregano.

Place in greased  casserole dish.

Cover and bake 350 degrees about 25
minutes  or until noodles and zucchini
are tender.

Uncover and stir, then sprinkle with
rest of cheese and bake uncovered until
cheese melts about 5 minutes.

Makes 4 servings


NOTE: You can peel zucchini if desired.

# ZUCCHINI & RICE

2 cups zucchini, Slice thin
1/2 cup Quick cooking brown rice
1/4 cup onion, chopped
2 tblsp parsley, chopped
1/8 tsp dried minced garlic
3/4 cup boiling water
1/2 tsp salt
3 eggs, lightly beaten
1/2 cup milk
1/2 to 3/4 cup sharp cheddar cheese
  grated


Combine zucchini, rice, onion, parsley, garlic, water and salt; Heat to boiling.

Cover and simmer slowly for 15 minutes.

Combine eggs, milk and cheese.

Add mixing slowly to zucchini mixture.

Place in shallow baking dish and bake 350 degrees about 40 minutes or until set.

# ZUCCHINI & CABBAGE

2 tblsp cooking oil      1/2 tsp sugar
1 tblsp onion, minced    pepper to taste
1 cup Zucchini, thinly sliced
2 cups cabbage, thin sliced & packed
salt to taste

In deep fry pan heat oil; Saute onion
few minutes.

Add cabbage, zucchini and stir well.

Sprinkle with sugar, pepper and salt.

Also, may sprinkle with minced dry
garlic if desired.

Stir and continue to fry until zucchini
and cabbage are slightly tender.

Cook about 10 minutes.

Serve hot with pork.

# STEWED TOMATOES

In saucepan combine; 2 cups canned
whole tomatoes, 1 tblsp minced onion,
1 tsp parsley, 1/8 tsp salt, 1/8 tsp
sugar, dash of pepper, 3/4 cup Zucchini,
thin sliced.

Bring to boil and simmer until zucchini
is tender.

Serve hot over toasted bread cubes.

# SALMON & CHEESE ON ZUCCHINI

8 oz cream cheese
2 tsp prepared horseradish
3 oz smoked salmon, finely chopped
1 tsp dill weed

Zucchini


Trim ends from Zucchini; cut in half lengthwise.

Place in boiling salted water to cover.

Simmer about 7 minutes or until barely tender.

Rinse in cold water and drain on paper towels.  COOL.

Beat cheese, horseradish and salmon until smooth.

Add dill weed and mix well.

Spread on cut side of Zucchini.

Cover and chill at least 1 hour.

Cut into 1" lengths to serve.


BY:

Blanche Westberg
Eugene, Oregon

# APPLESAUCE

2 cups Zucchini          1/4 cup sugar
2 cups apples            1/2 tsp salt
1/2 cup water
2 whole cloves
1 tblsp lemon juice
3/4 tsp cinnamon
1 tblsp red cinnamon candy


PEEL and cut up the apples and zucchini.

IN LARGE saucepan bring to boil:

    The Zucchini, apples, water, sugar,
    candy, cloves and salt.

REDUCE heat and cover... Simmer 20
minutes.

Remove lid and continue cooking until
liquid has evaporated.

Discard cloves.

Mash mixture and add cinnamon and
lemon juice.

Stir mixture well.

Store in refrigerator.


NOTE: If not used within a few days
      place in freezer cartons and
      freeze until needed.

# HOW TO ORDER ADDITIONAL COPIES OF THE

# "ZUCCHINI LOVERS COOKBOOK"

FOLLOW PRICES BELOW FOR AMOUNT OF BOOKS.

SEND CHECK OR MONEY ORDER ALONG WITH
YOUR MAILING ADDRESS TO:

## ADDIE'S RECIPE BOX
DRAWER 5426-Z79
EUGENE, OREGON 97405

1 book $5.65 - 2 books $9.99
3 books $14.50  ALL POSTPAID

If you would like to sell these cookbooks
please request FREE DEALER INFORMATION.

Volume prices available. WRITE TO ADDRESS
ABOVE: